PRAISE FOR *DIFF*

To go back "is a verb conjugated in dreams", Lauren Alleyne writes ... her debut volume *Difficult Fruit*, inscribing the governing mystery of this work, the secret knowledge of the dead. In anaphoric bursts of incantatory disclosure, in ghazals of love and survival, eros and the infinite, she does, indeed, go back, past all griefs and illuminations, "to the song beneath the song". There is uncommon spiritual knowledge here as well as political discernment. There is much to learn while accompanying Alleyne on her "raft of language" through a troubled world and an imagined heaven, to the place "from which comes all singing". I have gone with her and would do so again and again.

— Carolyn Forché: *The Angel of History*, *Blue Hour*

These "lyrics lay bare the marrow," examine an interior life and dreams, then turn their faces outward to the world with messages of celebration, cultural displacement, the transport of temporal sensation and the torment and regret of violence and self-destruction.

— Alison Meyers, Executive Director of Cave Canem

Lauren Alleyne's voice is a revelatory and formidable fusion of irrepressible music and uncompromising craft. Like snippets of cinema, these poems arrest the senses and challenge what's known. Every door this exceptional work opens opens onto a larger light.

— Patricia Smith: *Teahouse of the Almighty*, *Blood Dazzler*

In a masterful and sure poetic voice, a stunning debut, Lauren Alleyne takes us through the milestones of a life – from the vulnerabilities of a woman facing the pressures of forming her own identity, to what it means to be a person of difference, to what it means to journey through a culture with racial profiling. At the same time, Alleyne shows us what it means to love, to become engaged in a life of passion – directed not only toward a single person but toward the world at large.

— Mary Swander, Poet Laureate of Iowa:
The Girls on the Roof

Difficult Fruit is a book I wish there were no need for. But need there is, and Alleyne delivers poems of loss and grief and, thankfully, hope. "Meaning is the closest we get to salvation,/which is to say the word changes nothing/ – it does not unmake the rivers," she writes. But addressing the ages in ghazal and crown and free verse forms, she reminds us, in the "flaming sentence", that in one's life "it is in the raft of language we begin our escape."

— Lyrae Van Clief-Stefanon: *Black Swan*, *Open Interval*

DIFFICULT FRUIT

LAUREN K. ALLEYNE

DIFFICULT FRUIT

PEEPAL TREE

First published in Great Britain in 2014
Peepal Tree Press Ltd
17 King's Avenue
Leeds LS6 1QS
UK

ISBN 13: 9781845232276

Supported using public funding by
ARTS COUNCIL
ENGLAND

CONTENTS

I.

II.

III.

there is an amazon in us.
she is the secret we do not
have to learn

— Lucille Clifton, "Female"

ASK NO QUESTIONS,

Love, the door inside me is locked
and the bones are begging to be let
loose with their drums and handbells,
with their tales of the sea at sunrise.
I confess to the carrying of secrets.
I confess to bearing songs
not meant for your tongue. Some longings
are too heavy to move; others,
too spiked to cling to. Leave
the unused to their dusty sleep –
I have learned to live well enough
without them. Let me wring
my occasional tears, and stare
from time to time into corners
in which you see no incense.
Let me unbury my gods in secret
and rebind to them my prayers,
my necessary guilt. Let me believe
my happiness complete: this body
with your name on its gate, this deaf heart
that burns and shines and keeps on
turning the key.

TALKING TO THE DEAD

After Marie Howe

The poet says it began as a letter
to her dead brother, the poem
telling the last details of his life,
until she heard his voice whispering
I know. And what she wants to say
is that when we talk to the dead
we really mean to talk to anyone
who will listen, who will let us tell
our suffering and make it a story
with a beginning, a middle, an end.
And maybe it is about audience,
about which attentive air will receive
our insistences. All week, in the news
a dead boy's face, his final screams
replayed. All week, the solemnity
and ceremony of Easter, the lilies
on my makeshift chapel trumpeting
their fragrant declarations. The stories
told over and over – their protagonists
dragged up to act out their dying
until we tire of our incomprehension,
the proofs we invent that cannot satisfy.
Because the question is always *why?*
and the answer is unreachable –
lodged outside the realm of the living.
Because only the dead can say *I know*.

GRIEF ETCHES ITS SILVER INTO OUR DAYS, SINGING
9/11/10

What do the living owe the dead?
What tribute, what memory, what kingdom,
What time, what flesh, what fiction, what will,
What mourning, what missiles, what flag,

What dust, what patriotism, what purging,
What tears, what wick and wax and wavering
Light, what vigils, what sirens, what capital,
What codes, what questions, what mercy,

What protest, what burning, what god,
What terror, what blood, what wrath,
what drafts, what suicide, what occupation,
What pipelines, what desert, what hate,

What brotherhood, what target, what bomb,
What dignity, what sacrifices to their lingering
Ghosts, what stakes to scorch the guilty,
What guilt, what pleading, what prisoners,

What speeches, what revolution, what marches,
What jury, what freedom, what is left for us
To give them, what constitution, what tower
Do you wait in, O nation of martyrs, what anthem

To salute you, what convoy, what genocide,
What soldier, what search, what hidden silver,
What hostage, what amber alert, what bare feet,
What debt, what deliverance, what promises

To be kept, which to be broken, what purpose,
What redemption, what history, what ritual,
What bridges, what answer, what love, what
Love, what, living, do we owe our dead?

EIGHTEEN

With thanks to Frances Driscoll for the word

Tonight you are full of small rivers:
your eyes' salty runoff, the rust-bright
trickle staining your thigh, the unnameable,
undammed flooding in your chest –
you are drowning in all of them. Sweet girl,
of course you do not have the words –
it will take you almost ten years to find them;
they are both more powerful, and less
useful than you can believe in this night
when your hands and faith have failed you,
when your mouth is an absence of screams.
Some rivers are wider than any courage.
I give you nothing as you sink, alone
under those waters. This is how I am born.

*

Under those waters, you labour to birth me:
For days, you are dead to alarms, knocks, rings,
messages with their battery of concern
and questions you have no answer for.
You have made yourself impenetrable
to insistence with sleep's shadowy armour,
with a silence that consumes all sound
whole. You are beyond the world's reach,
which is one kind of safety. I can only imagine
that bodiless place, its darkness like a sweetness
in the mouth. The secrets you learned there
delivered me – your miracle scream, your dark
voice. Together, we left that realm of smoke,
returned to this country of blood, awoke.

*

You wake up, but you can never return.
No matter what country you burden
with dreams of home, if there are rivers,
if blood or tears or time flow there, if memory
lives or is buried there, if leaving was your own
doing, if you were captured or borrowed or lost,
if the doors were cast wide, or if you pried
them open, if there are doors, or doorways –
your name is not a key. Return has no means
in any language, no lines around it on any map;
To go back is a verb conjugated in dreams,
that dissolves on your tongue when you wake up
reaching for it. You seek a different debt,
choose a different peace: your verb, *to forget*.

*

And you forgot. You moved though your days
easy, with lightness that was not untrue.
You lifted weights and danced; you biked and ran –
you moved and moved, never still long enough
for your shadow to settle. You visited
familiar countries (not quite the same
as returning), made home the body's wild
contours. You wore short skirts and spiky heels.
You held bottles to your mouth, sparked fire
to your face, learned to suck the smoke in
and feel it swirling there next to your heart.
You defied sleep, worked the late shift at bars
instead of dreaming. You kept your eyes open,
your gaze fixed ahead on the slippery horizon.

*

O slippery horizon, seeming fixed,
just within reach is your most perfect trick.
You keep us going by it – hang your dazzle
like the perfect carrot; we chomp and chomp
toward you. When you're bright enough we need
never look behind; who wants to reach back
when the future beckons – a kept promise?
Eighteen, you know everything is at stake:
your possible life, hopes of making good
you long to realize, some nagging truth,
your sanity, pride. It is not a choice,
this horizon, but a bearable path.
We have faith in the signs saying *This way
to happiness: you are closer each day.*

*

You believe happiness is the bearable
vision of yourself: the woman who lives
certain in her skin; the woman who walks
unafraid, whose throat out-thunders thunder.
Each day she unwinds the bright rope of her
will, harnesses the hours for her pleasure.
Her laughter is an open door. Happy,
her heart empty of longing; happy is
her dreamless and unvisited sleep.
She is a bullet, a bird – all things swift
and light that ride on wind. She will not turn.
She will answer to no name but her own.
She is entire. She makes herself wide
so nothing can hold her; she holds all inside.

*

We hold all, 18. But not everything
dies because we believe burial an end.
Something waits to make gardens of us,
to wreath us with quiet thorns. It grows fat
and bursts its skin in us, thrives on our rivers;
it waits in our dark. It sets down roots, long
fingers probing the earth of us. It breaks
free and breathes the air of us. It reaches
for our light. 18, it creeps along our paths;
it thickens; it clings. *Inside our bodies*
something always waits to disappear, to burn,
or to startle us with bloom. It unfolds
obscene flowers: a doom of petals litters
us, our breath – their fragrance – heavy, bitter.

*

For years they scent our daily air, heavy;
breath after breath, we press on. The story
ripening in us, its eyes looking through ours
in the mirror. We have not seen our face
without its shadow for almost ten years,
and now this. In a class on *Violence*
Against Women, the professor prophesies
this moment – *it will come for anyone*
who has suffered trauma. We do not believe
we are *anyone* until we are sobbing
for the night that the boy you liked held you
down and made you bleed. Again, the rivers.
But this time I come bearing a word: *rape.*
We cling to the raft of it, begin our escape.

*

In the raft of language, we begin our escape:
We hold ourselves tightly inside it, whisper
its single syllable like a spell. The word
means it was not your fault for liking him,
for kissing him, for leaning into the touch
he pressed against your shoulders. Despite
your desire, despite the first thrill, the word
means you said *no*, too, and that matters.
The word tells us you were not being punished
by God. The word means you were not weak,
not stupid, not damned; you were a victim –
not a tease, not a cautionary tale or a moral.
This is what a word can give: definition,
meaning – the closest we can get to salvation.

*

Meaning is the closest we get to salvation,
which is to say the word changes nothing
– it does not unmake the rivers, cannot
erase them from the landscape of us – spells
have their limits. Which is to say return
means too-late-to-be-saved in any language.
*The longing is to be pure; what you get is to be
changed.* 18, we will carry our dark, we will
birth ourselves again and again; we will
tend our gardens, harvest the difficult fruit;
we will apprentice ourselves to the work,
and learn the language that will allow us
to summon our own angels. We survive;
we go on; we cross those rivers – we live.

IF, SKY

Wish for a working machine
and you're given a body.
Ask for options and you get
a life with no roadmap and
free will. Say, *Give me a reason*,
and what you get is silence
or wars continents too far away
to care without exertion.
If you say yes to knowing,
dispossession flowers in you,
and cleaves to your progeny
for centuries. If you wish
to forget, there are pills
with mild side effects –
dreams that grab you
by the throat and pockets
of fear that separate you
from your skin. If you sing
hymns the gods of memory
might waken and strike you
with elegies for your unguarded
heart. Ask for love, and the sky
will unveil itself layer by layer,
its naked blue flame wanting
only your blindness in return.

THE PLACE OF NO DREAMS

After Jamaica Kincaid

Is a cave so dark that every ghost shines
with the luminescence of super novas.
Wish upon every one, and you would
want for nothing.

The cave is a house with seven windows
and no doors.

The house of no doors is not lacking
an entryway, you have only to open
your imagination. Sometimes
a wall is a fear so old it has become brick.
Sometimes a wall is a wish so fragile
it would crumble if you uttered its name.

The name is a ghost offering
every possibility to the dark: a shining thing.
The name is an echo, is a mirror,

a corridor of clocks between now
and no time.

Now is a single drop of rain
hurtling towards a river.
The river runs, like all rivers – on.

At the mouth of the cave,
in the belly of the house,
at the edge of every hunger, the river
runs on.

Ghosts drink from it.

HOW IT TOUCHES US

For Anjane Maharaj

Our teacher trembled at the board as she unravelled
the snarl of events: exhaustion, a nap, the sickening
realization. Our friend was in a coma. We'd gawked

at lunchtime around Anjane's desk, shuddered at her
calm as she loaded up the insulin, flicked the needle
and slipped it beneath her skin, its live blue tracks.

I remember thinking I couldn't bear to live like that
but day after day when her chair remained empty,
I prayed she would come back to her body. Once,

we'd worked together on a project, about the universe
and its parts – planets, stars, atmosphere, black holes.
I couldn't remember which of us had kept it afterward.

The whole class went to the funeral, young and sombre
in our crisp collars and dark overalls. We shuffled past
the coffin; she lay white-faced and red-lipped as a doll.

The pyre waited at the river, its rough frame wreathed
like a wedding car with marigolds and loud red hibiscus.
Our teacher said we didn't have to, but we followed her

into the crowd gathered on the bank. The fire flung sparks
like little stars. When the pundit lit the torch to the wood
her mother's wails rose, first a tired thread, then heavier,

in thick, tangled knots of grief. When her body moved
I was unafraid; I thought we would witness a miracle,
that she'd get up and walk through those flames grinning.

But the motion was mechanical – her muscles stirring
as the tendons and ligaments contracted – a reaction to
the heat. That was all. No act of God. No resurrection.

Instead, the bang: her skull shattering, no longer able
to contain her brain as it expanded; the awful realization
that all laws of matter must hold true, and she was gone.

DEAR AUTUMN, THIS POEM TOO LATE,
REMEMBERS YOU –

You're the new girl.
Body turned away from the circle,
foot scuffing the floor,
you don't want to belong –
and who can blame you?
They're a ragged bunch,
the girls at the Center –
sullen, spaced out,
or screaming in corners
until the uniforms come
to shake the sound out
or muffle it with the rattle of pills.
But for an hour each week,
I come with my handouts
and books; we huddle over
ghazals, sonnets, haiku,
then tensed over your pencils,
you're supposed find your own words.
I'm here, you write,
because they want me
to tell them what he did.
But I'm not reading this
yet. I'm just watching
how your face seems so young
and so weary, your eyes
between flicker and fade
as you scribble into the notebook
you won't be allowed to keep.
I think poetry can save you,
but you're not interested
in poems – your reality
demands answers:
It's true, he touched me, but

I don't want him to go to jail.
He is a good person. He just needs
help. Miss Lauren,
you write, *what should I do?*
Your careful penmanship loops
and curves across the page,
its literal plea defying the break
of stanzas, metre, or line.
Home at my desk,
I discard note after futile note—
Dear Autumn, you're brave
and beautiful... Dear
Autumn, no one deserves...
the world is unjust... Dear
Autumn, have faith...
Dear Autumn, this poem... Dear
Autumn... I never get it right.

EIGHTEEN

Here is the night snarled with stars, here is the smile
full of teeth. Here is the bloom of desire, its scent swift
entering everything. Here are the arms, the legs, the heady
nectar of lips; here is nipple erupting against the thicketed
chest. Here is earlobe and thigh, the sharp seduction of nails.
Here is naked. Here, light by an exploring moon. Here is heat
making a new planet of your heart, riding your blood like victory.
Here is the old road you have longed and longed to travel.
It hisses your name. Its breath is smoke and salt; it stings
your throat like a scream. Here is the trembling gate, and yet
you want to turn back, no, run back, to before, which is still now,
or could be, if you turn in time and you do, but here are the knots
fists make of fingers, the silence one tongue can shackle to another,
the wilful iron of belly and bone. Here is *no,* and *no,* and no
answer. Here, shove and bite splinter like so much kindling.
Here is his laughter sparking mad – jackal, wildebeest, wolf.
Here is fire and fire and fire. Skins of flame. Walls of flame.
There is no turning here; here you learn how to burn.

ON THE MOST DEPRESSING DAY OF THE YEAR, JAN 24TH

for Shirleen

Its been proven, they say —
the bills like a line of ants,
the glamour of the new year
grown dull like a tin ring,
the dark taking the sky like a curve,
half the continent huddled
into scarves and sneezes —
the small engine of the brain
sputters and coughs, spins
the wheel of our brightness
to no avail. My friend tells me
she won't succumb, not this year,
that she's armed with a gadget
to simulate sunlight, to trick
her neurons like hothouse flowers
into defiant, artificial bloom.
It's her birthday, so I smile
but I can't stop the images
in my own untreated head
— dendrites sprouting threads
like untended ivy, brewing
storms of dopamine and serotonin,
everything out of kilter, ready
to blow. Her face looms over the cake,
the candles spelling the years
she has survived her own wild existence
— a flaming sentence, an almost-sun.
Her eyes squint their wish and flutter,
look at the light disappear.

JOHN WHITE DEFENDS

i.
They came
in the dead of night
with their ghost skin and war cries
their tongues sharpened with hate
    nigger this, nigger that
They came
as always they have come   and come
again   my worst nightmare sprung
alive – they were here
for my son

ii.
the fancy house
the two-car garage
the low trimmed lawn
the petunias and peonies
the tomatoes and summer herbs
my name in fancy letters on the mailbox

– I should have known
there would be a reckoning

iii.
I said, *please*   then
I said *stop*   then
I said *no*

iv.
I wanted
to spare him the burning
crosses
the dangerous
brotherhoods

the needle
the bullet
the shackles
the whip of a merciless law
I wanted to spare him
this

THE HOODIE STANDS WITNESS

For Trayvon Martin

I was built for bodies
like his, between boy and man,
sauntering in angles he couldn't hold
but swung his limbs from, careful
cool in every step.

I can tell you the story of him,
unexceptional –
he put change and candy
into my pockets, the necessary
jangle of keys and cellphone
hushed in the sock of me.

I watched him from the soft pile
he made of me on the floor
of his messy adolescent room
where I lay beside his sneakers
and backpack.
He did his homework
with chat windows open;
white headphones hooked
him into some steady beat.

That day, he was thinking
of nothing in particular.
He was quiet in his skin;
tucked into the shade of me,
he was an easy embrace
until an old ancestral fear
lay its white shadow
across us like an omen.

I can tell you his many hairs
raised in warning beneath me;
his armpits funked me up
with terror. His saunter slipped
into a child's unsteady totter
under the weight of a history
staggering behind him
mad with its own power.

He clung to me then, wholly
unmanned, a baby clutching
his blankey. He pulled me close
and I stroked his head, caressed
the napps he had brushed to waves
that morning. I felt him brace
his bones beneath me, his heart
a thousand beating drums.
The bullet ripped through us
like a bolt of metal lightning.
His blood, losing its purpose,
ran into me and I wished
we were truly a single body,
that I could have held
its rush and flow like a second
sweaty skin. I can tell you
how his spirit slipped out –
like steam from cooling water
– slowly, fading by degrees
until he stilled.

DEAR CHRISTOPHER,
After Joan Wickersham's *The Suicide Index*

You came home from work, slackened
your tie, slung your jacket across a chair,
and took the rope out of your briefcase.
You are a builder, and this is how you knew
the beam in the kitchen would hold you;
it is one you put in yourself, a foot thick.
The rope is as light as an idea, and maybe
the first few times you aim and throw,
it doesn't catch, and falls back to you
sighing *think, think, think, think*. But
you have had enough of thinking,
enough of the frayed nights spent
listening to everyone else's slumber,
enough of useless prayers and deaf gods,
enough of your wife's frightened eyes
following you around the house
and out the door every morning, as if
she could foresee the rope, finally
looping, the decision of the knot,
the chair from the new dining set
you drag into the room and stand on.
I don't know if you prayed before
you stepped off its plastic covering,
if you imagined forgiveness or punishment.
I am writing to tell you what happens after.
Your oldest son, twelve, comes home
first; he drops his backpack, goes for a snack.
It feels like days before he hears his mother
open the door and call for him. He wants to go
but he has wrapped his arms around your legs
and is pushing your slumped body up;
He is telling you over and over *It's okay,
Daddy, I've got you.* He wants you to know

he is strong, though his limbs are trembling
under your weight. *It's okay*, he chants.
Even after his mother finds him, runs
for a knife, and cuts your lifeless body down
he cannot let you go.

ELEGY

For Marlon André Collins, 1980-2010

Your dream was simple – to save
the world from moments like this,
abrupt calls and their dizzying
aftermath, the wild grappling up
and down the ladders of memory,
looking for answers, for trails
to follow to our own human comfort.
Marlon, the last time we met,
we were at an old man's funeral,
and the years of our old fallings out
dissolved in the waters of shared grief.
And now, it is noon on a spring day
months later, and you are dead,
your body abandoned in a hospital bed
where you left it after you grew tired
of doing what we are asked to do too often
on the sad and sunny island we call home –
wait to be seen.

Marlon, I am sorry you were alone
as the emergency exits in your body
sealed shut one by one by one,
as the infection flamed through
the kerosene trail of your blood.
You were burning, and no one heard
the alarms going off; no one saw
the smoke signals in your eyes.
No one pounded down the doors,
picked the locks or broke the windows.
Miles and years away we slept on.

Is it wrong to hope
a stranger asked you your name,
and held your hand?

Friend, I hope death was like a rescue,
that he came in a fireman's clothes
and carried you on his shoulders
out of that fiery house. I hope
that like Daniel in the lion's den,
the roaring terrors licked close
but never touched you. I hope
you made it out before the final explosion
closed your eyes to this imperfect world.

I hope you wake tended
by sweetness, with hands that feel
like home cradling your face,
that it is someplace where the light is cool
and without danger.

LOVE IN G MAJOR

Imagine heaven: the clean, unblinking
white of loose robes not much different
from the unifying Catholic school pleats
we despised as teens, our faces fresh, then
layered with adolescence, acne and angst –
even then we sang in choir: *What a friend
we have in Jesus*, and yes, it being heaven
I guess Jesus would be there too, and at last
we'd see those famous wounds up close,
ask what he thought of those tacky photos
of his Sacred Heart, with its thorny garland
and shouts of yellow light, a crimson star
afloat in the uncut cavern of his godly chest,
his robe still impossibly white, untouched
for all the bleeding such a heart must have
endured, but maybe we wouldn't discuss it,
since there'd be no more of that in heaven
– pain, I mean – rather, the body transfigured,
its annoyances abandoned, like moving out
of the cramped studio apartment, its broken
radiators, mouldy walls, cockroaches in the tub,
the heart, a bulging bag of trash left outside
for the dump truck to haul away, compact, bury;
and yes, love would exist, but as an accessory
– like the halo, fluffy wings, and sheet music –
it just comes with the gig, not earned, or lost
or given away haplessly, not the old monster
that stomps through this life devastating us
or the beguiling fairy that charms good sense
into sweet, burning madness – no, this Eden
is all serpent, no tongue; all tree, no desire
for more than the heady kiss of innocence,
and we are new again, first peoples – whole
amidst the unsullied bounty of the earth,
and we are not afraid, and we are not afraid…

39

THE EDGES OF THINGS
After Ann Carson

Without them, we are wind,
        flitting from body to body,
unanchored, in constant danger of our own
    sweet disappearance.

Take, for example, that night
        our bodies clung so close we became
a single longing – lip to whisper, burning
    to breast – how we took each other in

and in and in, our one skin slick, our sole
        mouth swallowing its inevitable air.
And how, though morning gave our bodies back
        you still whisper in me *Look, Love, I'm still here.*

LOVE IN A MAJOR
For Al

You wouldn't recognize this body of mine –
the odd animal it becomes
without you to answer its spark.
Here in the valley, I want nothing
but to heave the heaviness of my limbs
into the cocoon of my unmade bed
and burrow there, as if winter had come
and it was time, at last, for the long sleep.
When I think of sleep, I think of the way
our bodies tangle – my sweat, your sweat;
how my toes curl into the arch of your foot,
and you giggle even from the deepest of dreams.
I think of the way our dreaming tangles
with our waking – you turning over
in sleep to tell me of your dream banquet,
or the dogs rushing along a nameless river
and me, dazed by the fact of your body
beside me, the breaths I've come to
measure happiness by. This
happiness itself, a flowering, a hive of humming –
less a song, than the memory of song
from which comes all singing.

LOVE IN B MAJOR

Your hands, sturdy keys,
open in me a flock of doors:
I am endless entering.
My new name, *Consume me*.
You say *Let's*,
and our bodies twist into each other,
kisses bolting our mouths.
Nothing sounds like your voice
to which my every muscle tends.
Love, you are firm in me
– boulder, blessing, brick,
mortar, ruin.

LOVE IN B MINOR

Your sandbag body. Your blank moon eyes.

Your glasses a train derailed across your nose.

Your legs folding like bendable straws.

The empty bottle of bourbon rolling beneath

the bed. Our bed behind us, a wreck of linen

and loving. I want to walk out the kitchen door

into the morning and scream at the stupid birds

to stop trilling their meaningless arias. I want

to fly into the trees and find a nest to fall out of

singing. Your ghost voice crumbling into static.

Your bird hands like plucked strings, aquiver:

Do not sing to me. I want to push you out of my heart,

and watch your long fall through its chambers

and valves until you are momentary – a blip,

an irregular beat. Your siren, *please*.

Your face an arrangement of pain. Your face.

CATCHING SPY

When you die and go to heaven,
you look first for your father, the spy.
On earth, he was a bonafide James Bond,
with informants he met at the coffee shops,
bookstores, and parks he took you to as a cover.

You were ten when he sat you down and told you
that the men upending your furniture
were checking the house for bugs —
you thought there might be roaches
waiting in your bed to crawl into your ear.

At almost forty you like your vodka
straight from the bottle. When you get high
or too drunk to stand or both, you talk
about the spy gene, the one you believe
you inherited from your father, the beautiful
man who loved you so much you cuddled
and read the *Times* together on the couch
even after you were all grown up.
How can I miss him after 15 years? you weep,
How could he have used me that way?

And I, too, catch spy like a nasty infection,
search the linen closets and kitchen drawers
for the vodka you believe will make you forget,
or take you to him, your father,
whose death you return to like a spun wheel.

I wonder if he wants to be found, up there,
or if in his new garb of the saved
he'll blend in — his halo like any other
circle of light, his wings no bigger,
his face wearing that unfiltered bliss

and looking now, so unlike yours
here on earth when you think of him
looking down.

THAT THE BODY WANTS

The blue fist of our longing unfurls finger by precious finger
  and though every pore should flower at the thought of you,

Love, we've lost even this: the biology of us, once so certain
  that my palms could recall the quiver of your thighs in sleep.

To have known so little of our temperability, of our bodies,
  how they could heave us through desire into dailiness. Love,

Our hearts are slow horses wearying across this distance
  and we can no longer linger here, in memory's darkening.

A GHAZAL IN ARMS

When you sleep alone, tucked like nerveless wings, your arms
pillow your dreaming head, and you're in her arms.

Her, home. Him, home. God, that flashlight in the dark, home.
Home, Mother's hand. Home: love's many spiked and tender arms.

Psalm: O fractile and cadenced world, you are worthy
to be praised. O poets, O heart, lift up your arms!

Einstein the octopus can unscrew jars of food;
not bad for a slug's cousin, but he's got *eight* arms!

The debt-collectors find your new address. At home
the sheriff's star on a letter, the law's long arms.

In elementary school, punishment was this:
offenders knelt on the floor, and held up their arms.

In the bible, God promises the Israelites
victory if Moses never lowers his arms.

Stones and arrows, to gunpowder and mushroom clouds:
Our true evolution? The production of arms.

The Trail of Tears, Hiroshima, Guantanamo:
History is written by the mightiest arms.

Michelle Obama's upper body is *to die
for*, tabloids say, *the first lady's right to bare arms...*

Fourth degree red belt, and moving hard toward black –
the body becomes your race toward secret arms!

Lauren, face it: you're not ready for love's quiet
settling, though it woos you with wide open arms...

WHEN THERE'S ONLY YOU
AND YOUR DUMBSTRUCK FLIGHT

True story: you're strolling
through Manhattan's heavy summer
haze; a lover's hands move you
by the small of your back
through the crowd. Nothing
feels like home: not the slow Sunday
light breaking everything into glow,
not the rubbery wheeze of basketballs,
not the sirens reddening the air,
not the mouth at your ear bouncing
each word *Wait. Till. We. Get. Back.*
Even the voices hissing *sin*
sheathe their tongues.

Only a liar could say
it's easy to live two lives
and not have one plot blunder
its way into the other.

Flash back to church: the sweet-faced
boy at mass robed in white.
Then to college, and his hosanna of kisses.
How you bent your knees for a different blessing,
and thought you'd live out your days
beneath his godful weight.

Clueless, one lover's fingers trace circles
through the rasp of your dress.
The other walks toward you now.

THIRTY

This morning, you start from a dream
seasoned with bourbon. Last night roils in your stomach,
funks your breath, aches. A message
lights your phone, asking, *Did you get home safe?*
And as you answer, *Yes,* you wonder
if this is all it means to grow up: you don't
learn sense. You still find yourself swirling
in a strange city in your reckless boots,
the hum and shudder of liquor driving your feet.
Still, your heart parades its glitter for would-be lovers,
dissolves as they install themselves
in other women's arms. What you learn
is how to exit with grace. Despite the dark,
the sputtering streetlamp that is your only moon,
you learn to believe the streets will unfold
in the right direction if you just start walking.
And when you find you can walk no further,
a man with a beautiful accent and a meter will appear
on his metal-hinged steed and whisk you towards whatever
place your weary mouth conjures. Call it home.
30, maybe older and wiser is just learning
how to put yourself in your own good hands:
that you will wake up snug in your solitary bed,
your favourite pyjamas soft against your skin,
your hair tucked into in its stocking cap,
a glass of water on the nightstand waiting
to slake your morning thirst.

TO MY LOVER'S PARTNER, UPON THEIR SEPARATION

After Anne Sexton
For M.M.

I.

    We were travellers
who met on a bridge
beneath which a river flowed
full, and.
    The light was such
that our bodies disappeared
briefly; our souls unguarded,
recognized.
    They wished to greet
each other in the old ways of soul
of which we know nothing:

    When they fell back
into the dark hull of the body –
that dumb machine, that thick,
fleshy fabric
    – our souls popped
their eyelid peepholes, saw each
other: limbed, torsoed, with breath,
and beating hearts.
               And there,
on the bridge, *touch*.

II.

Here is another story:

Hunger is a beast.
We were fodder, ginger-
bread houses before a bear
with a sweet tooth
and claws.

How we were devoured.
How we never stood
a chance.

You understand.

III.

Or, perhaps we are the beasts —
roaring and fucking,
our eager, ferocious mouths
tearing at every delectable
arch and pit —

O, beautiful claws.

IV.

Apologia:
    I wanted nothing
but to sip at your river
    and slip away.
Instead, I swallowed the beast.
    Sometimes it howls in your voice.

LOVE IN A FLAT

After Dean Young

Dean told us a story about Coltrane:
how one time in a recording, he hit
a wrong note – *a real clam*.
In the second take, he hit it again,
this time harder, longer.
The third time, it becomes the heart –
the sound all the other notes wrap themselves around,
a different understanding of the melody –
the song beneath the song: the stubborn beat
holding up the heaviness of flesh.

A GHAZAL FOR THE BODY

To reinvent: tiny feet, brooms of lash, dimples, bones like air,
a new skin and smile. To be wholly, a different body.

At mass this morning, the miracle: ceremony, belief,
the exquisite transformation, *Amen.* Bread becomes body.

Corpse, cadaver, carcass. Husk, shell. So many words for the dead,
you say. There is no synonym for this: the living body.

The man who lives upstairs has been vomiting all this morning;
through the vent we hear the blunt heaves, the anguish of his body.

Outside, the exfoliated trees; leaves scattered like skin cells,
or loose hair. How thoughtlessly we discard, O patient body!

Four pounds of breast tissue removed after surgery and you
are a new woman; wear like new clothes, your rectified body.

Nights: the dream of flying. A freefall unchecked by gravity's
deadlock desire. Then morning. Land. Earth holds fast this body.

Kizi means *stay put*, but I am yearn: full of drift, of leaving;
there is no voyage called return, I take only the body.

SEVEN

In this picture, your dress is burning
white, your veil engulfs your head
like lacy flames. Your Snoopy watch
flares red on your wrist, you clutch
your white handbag like a wish.
Little Christ-bride,
you are innocence embodied,
down to your white knee socks,
Mary Janes, and unpierced ears.
Your parents are stiff with pride,
their afros not yet streaked white with worry.
Behind you, your godmothers hold fast
to their vows and your shoulders –
Nenny George, alive and beaming,
Aunty Patsy whispering into your ear, real
as the statue of Mary in the background.
Everything in this moment is true,
but even truth is not impervious to time,
and we lose so much – even this day's
memories will thin and disappear.
But you already sense this,
the anticipation already giving way
to something else you cannot name
as you solemnly wait to be captured,
bending your smile into the camera's light.

WHEN THE ANGELS COME,

After Roger Bonair-Agard's Burial Instructions For the Lovely Death

Let them bring wings.
Let the wings be poems
exquisite with the give
of each iamb. Let the music
be a harmonic of steel
pan and surf, congo drum
and Cher, my godmother's
shaky soprano and the sweet
thud of flesh falling away.
Let my thousand selves sing.
Let me tug my loved ones' coats
and let them catch me
in the afternoon's solitary
star. Let the dead make way
with hallelujahs. In their rain voices,
let them whisper to me.
Let each lived moment of love
light a path from this world to the next.
O Gods, when you call me
in all the names I have worn
through with breathing,
let me answer with joy;
let me go up, let me go
dancing, ecstatic with flight.

SILENT DANCES

Outside, snowflakes hurtle toward earth
like fat, determined birds.
But the wind derails their intent,
makes a gorgeous ballet of their frustrated march.
Inside, I turn the fire off an on again,
my body at war with equilibrium –
toasting then freezing. I stare out at the world
draping itself in February's late white,
the roadways shouldering each white feather.
What is the world, anyway? The crowd of white
building against anything that stays?
The cars lined along the curb, neat as flowers
in their beds? The flames billowing
at my feet that die without ceremony
with the touch of a switch? Half of me wants
to run out into the swirling, to join the thwarted
flakes in their solemn and whimsical dance.
Half of me grumbles, thinks of shovels and salt,
leaks and ice patches – the potential for damage.
In the distance ploughs have begun, their drag
haunting the silence. The train whistle
chimes in, then the traffic slushing past.
Then, quiet again. A different kind – one that has known
cargo and trees and the snowy commute home.
The kind that makes me flip the switch on
again, and off again, as I turn, warming
my body like a small world.

LETTERS TO JOHN RAMBO:

i.
Dear Rambo,
After all these years, you're back:
The muscles on your forearm bulging
as ever; the asymmetry of your face,
its trademark scowl; the rusty grate
of your voice reminding us – you're a man
who understands words don't matter
if you speak kickass.

ii.
Dear Rambo,
You've seen it all:
the way the body empties
like an icetray, the bullet's kiss
so clean it could break your heart,
the crimson fountain a wound makes –
wondrous in its puncture and spurt.
Beautiful, wouldn't you say?

iii.
Dear Rambo,
You've pushed your own body past
the recognizable limits –
the machine of your fist and eye sleek
and practised, ready to fire on command.
I know a man who died from cellular mutiny,
the cancer conquering organ after organ
until every cell turned renegade, ignored
the ceasefire he cried out in his sleep.
You must never worry about such things.

iv.
Dear Rambo,
If I ever paint you, it would be clay
on canvas. I'd put a fence in the centre
right where your heart would be.
I'd sketch your face and cover it with sand.
You'd be invisible: I bet you'd like that.
I'd add something to your portrait
every couple years, so rest assured
there'll always be a sequel.

v.
Dear Rambo,
I am so jealous of your metabolism!
I bet you never have to count calories
and can drink as much whiskey as you want.

vi.
Dear Rambo,
The last time I saw you,
I must have been ten. You were hot then,
but now, my heart is well-behaved
and does not even twitch at the sight of you.
I assume this means one of us has grown
too old…

vii.
Dear John,
we've known each other
our whole lives. I know
nothing fazes you.
Tomorrow I will be 29,
and frankly, John, I'm scared.
Tell me, what is the secret of fearlessness?

ODE TO THE BELLY
After Sharon Olds

You who I grab in disdain, your dark
dough spilling from my hands;
mark of the Buddha and Budweiser
– shame-maker, you. Belly,
you are the dictator of fashion,
demanding loose dresses, roomy
waistbands, rejecting swim suits
that expose. You are what I am measured by,
in your fullness, my lack. You, melon.
You, swallowed, unspinning globe.
In my dreams I am free of you –
I wear bikinis, do back flips, touch my toes;
but then I wake up wanting
to cram the world into my mouth
and let it fill you to bursting.
O, proud belly, you are the life-basket,
bearer of the thousand possible births.
You are birthday cake and wedding
toasts, fistfuls of buttery first-date
joy, you are pints of Dulce le Leche
scooping up the shards of my heart.
You are my father's bread on Christmas
morning, potatoes slow-cooked in ham fat
marking the New Year's plenty, you are
American apple pie, border burritos,
curried chicken with the skin on,
and Colonel Sanders' eleven blessed herbs
and spices. You are each day's necessary moon,
the house of singing, the cavern of bliss, the price.

GRACE BEFORE MEALS

Bless us, O Lord, and these thy gifts
which we are going to receive from thy bounty
through Christ, our Lord. Amen

As a child, I'd refuse to eat my veggies,
pushing them round and round my plate
until my mother's glare unclamped my jaw
and I choked down every last leaf.
Think, she'd say, *of the starving children.*
Ethiopia was big then – the television
haunting us with its images of thin limbs
and distended bellies, flies ringing
the faces of people too tired to brush them off.
How I'd wished I could slip the greens,
those healthy abominations, into the screen –
imagined the surprise of some little boy
when he saw my hand reaching down
from his sky passing the carrots and okra
like manna. In today's news, another riot
– in Haiti this time. Bands of people storm
Port-au-Prince, fearless with hunger
while peacekeeping troops place their guns
and bodies between the mob and the giant
containers of food stockpiled in the city.
I'm on my way to Wegmans; it's Monday
night and the parking lot is almost empty.
I pull my cart from the long train, discard
the one with the squeaky wheel. It's eerie
wandering alone in the fluorescent glow
to Bon Jovi, and the night manager's pen
clicking in time against his clipboard.
I walk right past the sprinkled produce,
wheel through the isles of fresh and frozen
meat, blocks of cheese waiting to be cut,

63

the twenty different types of cereal
high fibre/all natural/calcium enriched,
and for a second, it is a bad dream –
I'm in a labyrinth I must eat my way out of,
the ghosts of all the world's hungry
up in the bleachers watching, bony hands
under their chins, and the flies, again, the flies.
I roam the shelves, read their bright tags,
pick up or leave the cans and jars, the boxes
that read a complete meal in 10 minutes –
stock up to satisfy next week's hunger.
At checkout, the sleepy cashier offers paper or plastic,
piles bag after bag, and I pay with nothing
more than my name.

LETTER TO AUNTY PATSY

I can hear your laugh, the breathlessness
you'd clamp your hand around,
your shoulders working up and down like wings.

You were my first lavish crush.

The promise of summers in your new country
dulled the edge of your leaving for America,
where everything was made, and it snowed.

For years we yelled *Bye bye Aunty Patsy!*
every time a plane passed over the house,
those mysterious birds, night's unsteady stars.

Now, I am here in the country I labelled yours
before you disappeared – before the envelopes,
their stamps like trails, stopped brightening

the mailbox, and birthday bills tucked into singing
cards no longer made their way to our piggy banks.
Gone, the hearts above the flourish of your name.

For two decades I've imagined you here:
your face hidden behind the *Times* on the subway,
your fingers dropping change in every hungry cup.

Before you left, you whirled me
around the living room until we collapsed,
giggling; we chanted the months until I would come to you

like prayers. You've saved our pictures.
You wait and wait for me to find you.

10 MOST SACRED SPOTS ON EARTH

1

The patch of lawn
beneath the backyard tree
where you turned your first soil,
laid your first seeds and hopes,
that you bless with your watching.

2

The bathtub: made and installed
circa 1925. It holds the whole
of you and bubbles, beside...

3

In the flat centre of an archipelago's
southmost island
a house with a set of stairs
that leads nowhere awaits you.
Climb them, and look up.

4

The after-hours silence
of the office. A chair that knows
your shape too well.
Your fingers flying at the keys.

5

If you lay a candle on the shore
the whole ocean
is made holy.

6

The birthmark on your lover's chest,
worthy of pilgrimage.

7
Is Oz on earth?

8
Blood-blessed Jerusalem —
its sand-seared deserts; the cutting light.

9
Four naked women stand waist-deep
in the Aegean, laughter unchained
from their throats. They consecrate the sea.

10
Beside your kitchen sink, a sprout
breaks through soil into air
and wonder takes root in you.
The world awaits your blossoming.

FOURTEEN

How the bud yearns to flower
believing that bloom is all
beauty, perfuming, the bliss
of pluck. How she knows nothing
of uprooting, the constraints of glass,
the burden of perpetual brightening.
When she blossoms in her dreams
she is only the full rose of herself,
free at last from the inconvenient
root. How she strains against
her greenness, prays for the day
a hand will lift her away. Ah, rose.
Let us not tell her of wither.
Let her turn her best face to the sky.

LETTER TO THE OUTSIDE
Jentel, WY May 2008

It is magic here, outside the rule of clocks and scurry. The vast baskets of mountains overflow; the clouds clink like ice in a glass: I drink it all in, and it is enough. What a concept, contentment. Yesterday, where the creek tipples at the base of the valley, I saw a dead goat — stiff, ringed with flies, its face like a plate of leftovers. I wept, then I did not. I stood at the roadside until the wind wafted up its benediction. From this place I gift you the unoccupied air; the wobbly prancing of new calves; a sky so close the stars might be a chain-link fence you run your hands along as you amble through the night; your live and mutable body, its spark and spell and solitude. Write back.

THE X-RAY

I feared and revered it,
this black and white portrait
pinned calmly against the harsh

fluorescent glow, the cryptic stare
of my doctor in her white lab coat,
her ballpoint pen briskly outlining

the skeleton of my wrist: the fragmented
carpals; the rivers of dark separating
the tiny pieces of the metacarpals;

the four long fingers, their bony white
columns; the nebulous lumps of each
knuckle, speed bumps on a curving road;

the comparative stub of the thumb,
the thick layers of adipose transformed
into a barely visible greyness.

It did not apologize, demur, or cower
at our scrutiny – it dared us, even,
to look deeper, to pick each tiny layer apart,

dig through the thick cartilage,
the grain of ligaments, the ivory-coloured
coating, to lay bare the marrow, the blue veins,

the dark arteries, and thin capillaries
rich with plasma and blood cells
on their journeys to and from the heart.

I have longed to live like this:
to be held up to the light, naked
beneath any official stare – found whole.

FIFTEEN,

I am writing from 29 to tell you
we live. I remember our dreams,
the long white halls with no end,
and how when we tried to imagine
life after high school, it was blank
and solid as a grave. We thought
that meant there was no future
for us, and practised accepting
our absence from our own lives
– no more best friendships, school
dances, no more yearning for boys
to whom we were already invisible.
Now, we are almost twice your age.
The face we couldn't envisage is yours
but leaner, with shadows of Mom
in its profile. In two years, we will
step on our first plane, and fall
in love with flight. We will move
like wind across the world: we
conjugate French class verbs in Paris
and Nice; we follow Jesus to Bethlehem,
and Galilee; we have lived in places
you do not yet know exist. I see now
that it will all begin with you –
the path away from home marked
with nothing; who could walk it
but the girl who has already made peace
with her own end? 15, looking back,
I understand our quiet death-wait,
the surprise of our persistent, daily waking:
We never could have imagined this.

NOTES:

p. 14: "Eighteen"

Frances Driscoll's *The Rape Poems* should be required reading.

p. 17: "Inside our bodies something always waits to disappear, to burn, or to startle us with bloom" is from Ada Limón's poem "insert" from her book *Lucky Wreck.*

p. 18: "The longing is to be pure, what you get is to be changed" is from Jorie Graham's poem "Prayer" from her book *Never.*

p. 27: "John White Defends"

John White is an African American who was convicted for shooting a young white teenager who went to White's Long Island home at 2 a.m. drunk and armed with a baseball bat, claiming that he and his posse were there to "take care of" White's son, Aaron. The white teen was upset because of a rumour that Aaron had made sexual comments about the teen's (white) girlfriend on Myspace.

p. 29: "The Hoodie Stands Witness"

Trayvon Martin was shot and killed by George Zimmerman in February of 2012. Zimmerman reported seeing someone "suspicious" wearing a hoodie in his neighbourhood, and called the police. Ignoring the 911 dispatcher, Zimmerman followed and confronted Martin, and fatally shot him.

p. 48: "To My Lover's Partner, Upon Their Separation"

The poem takes as its inspiration Anne Sexton's "For My Lover Returning to His Wife".

p. 51: "A Ghazal for the Body"

there is no voyage called return is a phrase from the Syrian poet Ali Ahmad Said, also known as Adonis.

p. 61: "Grace Before Meals"

The epigraph is the Catholic prayer commonly recited before meals.

ACKNOWLEDGEMENTS:

Without the following people, journals and organizations, neither I nor this book would have come to fruition. You were my earth, roots, rain and sky.

My best friend and first reader, Catherine Chung.

My other wonderful readers and writing kin: Lisa Maria, Pilar (my star) Gómez-Ibáñez, Misty Rae Urban (of LaMzT), Dawn Lonsinger, Autumn Watts, Michael Simons, Erika Mueller, Rita Chin, John Murillo, Melissa Tuckey, Alice Oleson, Anastasica Tolbert, Krista Franklin, Mohanalakshmi Phongsaven, Karl Parker, Anne Owen-Shea, Thomas Sayers-Ellis, Roger Bonair-Agard. The Sirens of Serifos.

My teachers and mentors: Lyrae Van Clief-Stefanon, Mary Swander, Patricia Smith, David Mura, Carolyn Forché, Cornelius Eady, Toi Derricotte, Larissa Szporluk, Alice Fulton, Ken McClane, Stephanie Vaughn, Michael Koch, James Crenner, Katharine Whitcomb, Sheryl St. Germain, Debra Marquart, Tracy K. Smith, Alfred Corn, Brother Edward Wesley, Dr. Virginia Franklin, Terry Quinn.

The workshops, retreats and foundations that gave me the time, funding, and immeasurable support to write: Cave Canem, Yaddo, The Community of Writers at Squaw Valley, The Saltonstall Foundation, Jentel, Colrain Manuscript Workshops, Callaloo, The Fine Arts Work Center in Provincetown, The Dorothy Sargent Rosenberg Foundation, Split This Rock, A Room of Her Own Foundation.

The journals who offered many of these poems their first homes: *Connotation Press* ("To My Lover's Partner", "The Place of No Dreams", "Love in B minor"), *The Caribbean Review of Books* ("Ode to the Belly"), Blog This Rock ("Eighteen"), *Southword* ("How It Touches Us"), *Aspeers* ("Grace Before Meals"), *Cimarron Review* ("When There's Only You," "Ghazal in Arms") *Bellevue Literary Review* ("On the Most Depressing Day of the Year"), *No Tell Motel* ("Ask No Questions"), *About Place* ("10 Most Sacred Spots", "Silent Dances"), *Dublin Poetry Review* ("Grief Etches its Silver"), *G'Nat Magazine* ("If, Sky," "Dear Autumn," "Talking to the Dead"), *Aesthetica* ("Eighteen").

My Peepal Tree team for investing and believing in this book: Kwame Dawes, Jeremy Poynting, Hannah Bannister, and Adam Lowe.

DéLana Demaron and the team at Red Olive Creative Consulting for their work on building my website and promoting this book. Mih-Ho Cha for her sage advice.

My family, that bundle of sticks that cannot be broken; I love you all: Annette, Cornelius, Debra, and Ray Alleyne. Norma Rock, who is as steadfast as her name suggests. Aunty Marge, the strongest root.

The members of my other family, especially Kenneth Skerett, Reynold York, Jocelyn Sinnanan.

My cheerleaders near and far: Mandisa Greene for believing always. Kris Sealey, Dixil Francis, Stacey Molin, Jhosan Hyland, Meredith Mullane, Jenny Abbott, Kim Hilby, Alison Meyers, Rose, Edna Lawrence, Marilyn Hinkson, Janet Stanley-Marcano, Hayzel Braithwaite, and Sybil Davis who is a gift and a joy.

The gone ones, still beloved: Anton Stewart, Joan (Nenny) George, Aunty Queen, Uncle John, Elton Asson, Brother George Larkin, Marlon Collins, Miguel Bernal, Anjane Maharaj, Lucille Clifton.

I thank God for these and all blessings.

ABOUT THE AUTHOR

In 1997, Lauren K. Alleyne left her home country of Trinidad and Tobago to study Radiologic Science and Nuclear Medical Technology at St. Francis College, in New York. However, in her junior year, she became an English major, and graduated with honors with a B.A. in English. She went on to earn an M.A. in English and Creative Writing from Iowa State University, and a Master of Fine Arts in Creative Writing from Cornell University, where she also completed a Graduate Certificate in Feminist, Gender, and Sexuality Studies. Lauren is a Cave Canem graduate whose work has been widely published in journals and anthologies. She is the Poet-in-Residence and an assistant professor at the University of Dubuque.

2013 POETRY TITLES FROM PEEPAL TREE

Kadija Sesay: *Irki*
ISBN: 9781845232085; pp. 90; price: £8.99

Velma Pollard: *And Caret Bay Again*
ISBN: 9781845232092; pp. 188; price: £10.99

Raymond Ramcharitar: *Here*
ISBN: 9781845232047; pp. 64; price: £8.99

Edward Baugh: *Black Sand*
ISBN: 9781845232108; pp. 134; price: £8.99

Vahni Capildeo: *Utter*
ISBN: 9781845232139; pp. 78; price: £8.99

Sai Murray: *Adliberation*
ISBN: 9781845232061; pp. 72; price: £8.99

Malika Booker: *Pepper Seed*
ISBN: 9781845232115; pp. 84; price: £8.99

Roger Robinson: *The Butterfly Hotel*
ISBN: 9781845232191; pp. 72; price: £8.99

Jane King: *Performance Anxiety*
ISBN: 9781845232306; pp. 116; price: £8.99

All available online at peepaltreepress.com
or email orders to orders@peepaltreepress.com
or phone +44 113 245 1703